THE
Archive Photographs
SERIES

COOKHAM

An old cottage in Cookham High Street, *c.* 1895. There is no room in the bassinet for the baby as the boys pose outside their tumbledown house. It was demolished in 1896 and replaced by Southlands Cottages.

THE
Archive Photographs
SERIES

COOKHAM

Compiled by
Chrissy Rosenthal and Ann Danks

TEMPUS

First published 1998
Copyright © Chrissy Rosenthal and Ann Danks, 1998

Tempus Publishing Limited
The Mill, Brimscombe Port, Stroud,
Gloucestershire GL5 2QG

ISBN 0 7524 1113 6

Typesetting and origination by
Tempus Publishing Limited
Printed in Great Britain by
Midway Clark Printing, Wiltshire

This book is dedicated to Ben, Rebecca, Tom, Bryony and Alex.
Look after it!

An early engraving showing the Cookham Ferry crossing the Thames by Holy Trinity parish church.

Contents

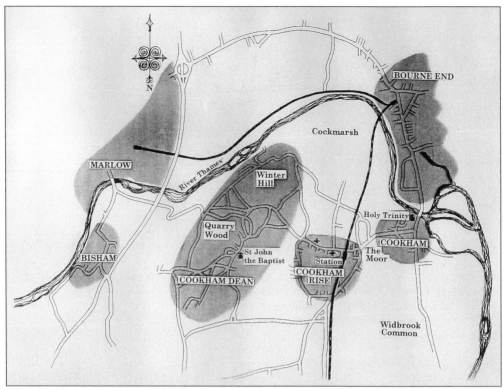

The three areas of Cookham – the Dean, the Rise and Cookham Village – are situated along one of the most beautiful stretches of the Thames. (Map by Gordon Badnell, 1998.)

Filling in the pond at Dean Farm, October 1901.

Introduction

'A village made in Heaven' Stanley Spencer called it – and local residents heartily agree. Cookham was put on the map by the artist and tourists come from around the world to see the village he made famous in his many and varied paintings. The name of 'Cookham' actually covers three distinct areas: Cookham Village with its beautiful old cottages and ancient church, Cookham Rise, home to the railway station, nursery school and shops and Cookham Dean, more rural and wilder in its history.

Sitting on a beautiful stretch of the River Thames, the area has always attracted visitors – from the Romans and Danes through to more modern times when the Great Western Railway brought day trippers to see the famous cherry orchards in blossom. Many other artists and writers have been inspired by the area. Among them was Kenneth Grahame, who lived in the Dean when he wrote *Wind in the Willows* and set it in our wild woods and river banks.

Cookham has for centuries been home to hard-working people. It still is – only the jobs have changed over time. There is evidence of an Iron Age settlement as early as 100 AD and there has been a church on the site of Holy Trinity since the Domesday Book was written. It has been both an important river crossing point and market town. Nowadays, although many people work locally at Maidenhead or High Wycombe, easy access to Paddington and good connections to the M4 and M40 make it a very popular place to live for commuters to London.

As with other modern villages, it has witnessed enormous change over the past hundred years. Nevertheless, Cookham seems to be surviving quite well. The acres of common land, now administered by the National Trust, have helped to define the rural landscape. Farming is still carried out, although as any modern farmer will tell you, economics clash with aesthetics most of the time. Many of the old families remain – although again the cost of living in such a pastoral paradise so close to London has pushed many house prices beyond local means.

The river has played an important part in our history, giving us strategic importance in the very early days and a source of income for fishermen and boatmen alike. It has also caused some devastating floods, evidence of which can been seen in this book. Industries have come and gone: the fruit farming is now almost exclusively pick-your-own and the basket making, shoe making, paper making and brick and tile manufacture have all gone. The fruit and vegetable shops, tobacconists, tea rooms and haberdashers have been replaced by boutiques, gift shops and restaurants, but Cookham thrives. Cookham Rise still has a parade of local shops which can provide for the needs of the community, although they are battling with big supermarkets for survival. We have our own nursery school and three flourishing primary schools. You can buy organic sausages, a wood burning stove, a bunch of flowers, a work of art, high class second hand clothes, a pair of knickers, an antique pot and even a pint of milk in Cookham shops. What more could you want?

We have been very greatly helped in our researches by two wonderful histories: one put together by Stephen Darby, published in 1909, and the other an unpublished history written by Brian Dodds, who died in 1958. Both these historians were meticulous in their record keeping, and have been a most useful source of dates and information. We have also been lucky enough to have seen stories written down by Norman Jordan and Jim Skinner, both full of fascinating insight into life for previous generations. Ray Knibbs wrote entertainingly of visits to Cookham Dean in the early part of the century and made us determined to find a photograph of Joe Tomlin's 'wonderful long' runner bean called 'Cookham Dean' – but we never did! There is much reading matter for those who want to study the history of Cookham.

This, however, is not a history book. It is a celebration of the collectors of Cookham, of which there are many. Those who have shared their treasures acknowledge how important it is to hand on these images to the next generation. When we learn of the ways of the past, we appreciate the present, and learn to look after the future. We certainly thank them all very much.

Many of the photographs in this book are from personal collections and have been seen by relatively few people. We hope you find them as fascinating as we do. Each one excites an appreciation of the way things were and also, we hope, a desire to maintain and preserve the best of what we still have. The costumes and modes of transport may change, but the 'good, hard-working folk' are still the same, and many of our beautiful buildings have been lovingly restored. The farming landscape has not escaped so lightly and the planners of the future must be encouraged to cherish what is left.

Many stories have been related to us from memory, passed on by parents and grandparents. Where we can we have added these to the captions and hope you enjoy the diversions. We would point out though that several of these stories have been contradicted by the next version - but then the memory can play tricks!

Royalties from this book will be going to help support Elizabeth House, The Day Centre for the elderly in Station Hill, Cookham Rise. This centre is a good example of how the Cookham community pulls together – the need was recognized and driven by Elizabeth Saunders, the money was raised and the centre opened. It is run by volunteer labour, cooks, cleaners and drivers. It is a wonderful facility that is appreciated by the whole community and we appreciate your help in supporting them by buying this book.

Ann Danks and Chrissy Rosenthal

If you have any other photographs or memories you would like to share with others then please phone 01628 482715.

Children posing by a favourite hiding place at Winter Hill, 1896.

8

One
Cookham Village

Cookham High Street, c. 1900.

Cookham High Street from Wistaria Cottage, c. 1930. On the right The Bel and The Dragon Hotel boasts a garage and next door Mr David Pryce-Jones advertises his services as the local chemist. The road turns back into a rural track as it winds into the Pound and up to the Rise.

View from Cookham Church Tower.

Cookham Bridge from the church tower, 1903. The weir and boatyards are still a familiar sight, as are the views across to Hedsor. In Taunt's 1878 edition of the *Illustrated Map of the Thames* he points out the recently built slim iron toll bridge and the panoramic countryside. The bridge replaced an old wooden structure that villagers were refusing to cross because of its condition.

Ovey's Farm in the High Street, *c.* 1892. Farmer George Hatch held regular 'smoking concerts' in the barn. At the annual meeting of the Quoits Club, after the business was rounded off, he was heard to sing 'A Rainy Day' and 'The flies be on the tur-me-yuts'. Many other villagers also joined in. Sir Stanley Spencer, the well known Cookham artist, was born in Fernley, the house across the road, and sometimes used the barn as a studio.

LLEWELLYN'S HOTEL.

CLOSE BELOW THE BRIDGE.

This Hotel having been extensively enlarged, offers superior accommodation to Anglers, Boating Parties, and others visiting this the finest part of the Thames.

Choice Wines and Spirits.

BOATS, PUNTS, & CANOES TO LET BY THE HOUR, DAY, WEEK, OR SEASON, ON REASONABLE TERMS.

JAMES LLEWELLYN, Proprietor.

Llewellyn's Hotel, advertised in 1878. The flag pole shows that the hotel was known as The Ferry, as it is today, and offered 'superior accommodation, and choice Wines and Spirits'. Band concerts were held on the lawn which led down to the river.

The Ferry Hotel, *c.* 1891. The staff pose with the new owner John Kilby. The black and white timbered building on the approach to the slipway has altered little despite many changes to the rest of the hotel.

The Royal Exchange, *c.* 1910. A horse-drawn delivery vehicle arrives at the pub. The proprietor, James Ware, kept a livery stable, the gates of which can be seen to the right. Judging by the bicycles outside it was a popular watering hole! These days it is an Italian restaurant.

The Kings Arms Hotel, High Street, *c.* 1910. It was during this period that regular concerts were held in the gardens on fine summer evenings. Back in 1668 for unknown reasons landlady Martha Spott issued her own coinage, a few examples of which still exist. Records show that in 1920 the pub changed hands for the princely sum of £77 18s 10d.

The Crown Inn on the Moor, *c.* 1893. Spectators enjoy watching an afternoon game of quoits. At this time Cookham United Quoits Club regularly held competitions and played for the Challenge Cup. This building was one of three public houses on the site, the first two of which were destroyed by fire.

The Crown Hotel, *c.* 1914. The second Crown on this site, it was also destroyed by fire. Advertised as a 'high class, bijou hotel close to the river and station', it burnt down in July 1926. The local paper tells a dramatic story of Dan the bull terrier arousing his master Harold Moxon – a 'resting' acrobat – from his sleep, who then escaped down knotted sheets! Telephone calls to the fire brigade went unanswered, so the Klofacz brothers who were neighbours leapt onto their motorbike and dashed the three miles to Maidenhead to get help. Residents who remember the fire tell how as children they lined up on the Causeway and listened to the corks popping out of bottles.

Keeley's Cottages, 1919. Cookham-born Kate Francis (now Swan) is seen here with family and friends. The Crown is on the left on the corner of Berries Lane. In the centre of the picture is Tommy Klofacz, the hero of the fire. From the left: Ferdie and Kate Francis, Thomas Klofacz, Eddie Pearce and Freda Klofacz.

A coach and four outside the same cottages.

Cookham High Street just before the First World War. In this peaceful scene there is little hint of the troubles ahead. The Tarry Stone can be seen at the top of the street, moved to this position in 1909. Note the evidence of horse-drawn transport on the road in the foreground!

The Tarry Stone is one of Cookham's relics. In the twelfth century it was a boundary marker for the Abbot of Cirencester's property. When the new bridge was built in 1839 it had to be moved and ended up in the Mill House garden. When this property came into the hands of the Youngs – a prominent local family – Sir George returned the Stone to the village. He can be seen here in his familiar Astrakhan coat supervising the move.

The Stone remained in position at the top of the High Street until 1936 when it moved yet again to its present site on the corner of Odney Lane, against the wall of Bridge House (now the Dower House). The bench was added in 1942 in memory of Pilot Officer Michael Briggs. Sadly his memorial inscription is now all but worn away.

The Tarry Stone, Cookham   CK 10

Cookham Church.

Holy Trinity Church, *c.* 1890. The church tower was still covered by a huge ivy tree which local boys would climb to collect the jackdaw eggs. They say it was fourteen inches round the trunk. The clock is only just visible, and the sundial and window are totally obscured. The church is an ancient building of sandstone, flint and chalk, with some parts dating back to Norman times. The wooden grave markers seen in the photograph are called jumping rails and these and the iron railings disappeared many years ago. The graveyard was closed to burials in 1899. Sir Stanley Spencer could often be seen painting in the churchyard and used it as the setting for his major work *The Resurrection*.

Church Corner Cookham.

Churchgate House, a half-timbered house which dates from the thirteenth century, but which has been modernized greatly since. A Victorian donkey cart stands outside one of the oldest buildings in Cookham. To the left is one of the most notable memorial stones in the churchyard – a winged angel erected in 1897. Churchgate Cottage is to the right.

Churchgate, an imposing Victorian building, stands opposite the church gates.

Sir Stanley Spencer in 1958. Setting up his easel, he is preparing to paint for a special exhibition which raised money for church funds. He is at the side of Churchgate, facing the church. The area is roped off to prevent curious onlookers from distracting him. Over the three weeks of the exhibition 25,000 people visited Cookham, and £4,000 was raised. Lord Astor bought *Listening in Punts* – part of the 'Christ Preaching at the Regatta' series – although sadly not in aid of church funds!

Sir Stanley buys Christmas gifts in 1957. He is at the newly opened Parish Centre in Church House, Cookham Road.

The toll bridge in the summer of 1947. Mrs Chainey collects one of the last tolls on Cookham Bridge. The notice advertises Maidenhead Regatta and the ten challenge cups to be won that year. At the ceremony to declare the bridge 'free', Captain H. Pinder-Brown remarked that 'this is the end of Cookham as we have known it. It will now become a village on a main road'.

The Cookham Bridge Company list of tolls in 1905. There is no price yet for motor cars, which were just becoming a popular means of transport among the wealthy. With the speed limit at 20 mph, the water cart was still needed to damp down the dusty roads. Villagers were already complaining about the speed, noise and pollution of the traffic and at one council meeting the motor car was dismissed as 'the rich man's luxury and the poor man's curse'!

COOKHAM BRIDGE COMPANY.
LIST OF TOLLS.
TO BE TAKEN AT THE BRIDGE Every Time of PASSING
on and after the 1st day of Sep.r 1905.

	£	s	d
For one Horse Mule or other Beast (except an Ass) Drawing a Carriage of any Description For the First time in any Day			6
For every additional Horse Mule or other Beast (except an Ass) Drawing a Carriage of any Description for the first time in any Day			3
For one Horse Mule or other Beast (except an Ass) Drawing a Carriage of any Description for every time in any Day after the First time			3
For every Additional Horse Mule or other Beast (except an Ass) Drawing a Carriage of any Description for every time in any Day after the first time			1½
For every Ass Drawing a Carriage of any Description for the first time in any Day			3
For every Ass Drawing a Carriage of any Description for every time in any day after first time			1½
For every Horse Mule Ass or other such Beast, Not Drawing			2
For one Cow, Bull, Ox, Calf or other Neat Cattle, Not Drawing			2
For every additional Cow, Bull, Ox, Calf or other Neat Cattle Not Drawing			1
For Sheep, Lambs, Pigs at the Rate Per Score			6
For every Foot Passenger or Person Passing over the said Bridge (other than such Person as shall bona fide belong to any Carriage Beast or Cattle chargeable-any Toll or Tolls) Having any Truck wheelbarrow or bicycle or other vehicle not chargeable with toll			1
For every other Foot Passenger or Person not actually and Bona fide belonging to any carriage, Beast or Cattle hereby Chargeable.			½
For every Carriage of whatever Description having not more than Two wheels moved or propelled by steam or machinery or by any other Power than Animal Power for the first time in any Day			3
For every such Carriage as last mentioned for every time in any day after the First time.			1½
For every Carriage of whatever Description having two and not more than three wheels moved or propelled by steam or Machinery or by any other than Animal Power for the first time in any Day			4
For every such Carriage as last mentioned for every time in any day after the first time.			2
For every Carriage of whatever Description having four or more Wheels moved or Propelled by Steam or Machinery or by any other than Animal Power for the first time in any Day		1	0
For every such Carriage as last Mentioned for every time in any Day after First time			6

Sutton Croft, 1892. The builder was Julius Spencer, Stanley's uncle, and it was commissioned by the Young family. The house stood in extensive grounds at the end of Mill Lane and was demolished in the 1960s to make way for new houses and the creation of Sutton Close.

Formosa, c. 1890. The home of the Young family was built by the first Sir George in 1785. He was an admiral and built the inside of the house to resemble a ship. The beautiful garden runs down to the river and in the 1920s it became the Cliveden Reach Hotel. It finally fell into disrepair and was pulled down after the Second World War.

Moor Hall, *c.* 1946. At this time it was run by Gaumont British Animations Ltd. It was used as a base for animated cartoons and film production. Built in 1805, it was a farm and became a 'gentleman's residence' at the end of the century. It has been very much extended and is now the headquarters of the Chartered Institute of Marketing.

The Elms, 1907. Note the effects of the major fire which severely damaged the home of Colonel F.C. Ricardo, a noted local dignitary. The recently formed Cookham Fire Brigade, under Captain H. Pinder-Brown, 'worked well' according to the Colonel who was their President! Previously this house was called Lullebrook Manor, and was once used as the base for the shoe manufacturing industry in the area. It is now the Odney Club, owned by the John Lewis Partnership.

Holy Trinity School, class two, in 1909. They are outside the corrugated tin hut which was used to hang up hats and coats. The headmistress at the time was Miss Mary Gibbins, and there were ninety-four pupils in the school.

Formosa Fishery, c. 1942. This house belonged to the Young family, and was close to their other property at Formosa. It spent some time as a hotel, but here it is the 'Formosa School for Boys and Girls', where the pupils appear to be enjoying taking part in a school play.

Two

Cookham Rise

Lower Road, Easter Sunday, April 1908. The milk delivery gets through despite a late Spring snow storm. Parts of the county had twelve inches of snow and arctic conditions were reported.

Cookham railway station, 1902. The stationmaster for the Great Western Railway was Mr Edward Wilder, second from left in front of the elaborate vending machines.

Cookham railway station. Opened in 1854, the railway was responsible for the quick expansion of Cookham Rise. At one point the problem of moving horse manure out of the streets of London was partly solved by transporting it by rail to the Dean farmers who used it to fertilize fruit trees. A Mrs Preston complained bitterly to the local paper about the health hazard this caused. A GWR surveyor was dispatched, and decided to enlarge the siding to unload the manure further away from nearby houses.

Cookham Railway Station

The railway sidings, 1902. A traffic jam builds up as the steam train puffs away towards Bourne End and the level crossing gates remain shut. Behind the now demolished signal box is The Working Men's Club and Reading Room which was erected as a permanent memorial to Queen Victoria's Diamond Jubilee. There were several fly cab companies in the village and the Dean, one of which was run by H.W. Jordan. Phaetons and horse-drawn carriages were a familiar sight.

The postmen collect in the snow outside the sorting office, 26 April 1908. Mr William Shergold was the sub-postmaster and the first delivery was at half past six in the morning.

Shergold's shop in Station Approach in 1915. Mr Shergold was not only the sub-postmaster, but had a nursery near the station and sold fruit, flowers and stationery. He was soon to open a second shop in Cookham High Street.

Southview Cottages in High Road, known locally as the Top Road, when they were newly built. The boys are posing in their Sunday best stiff collars. The unmade road leads on to Kennel Lane and up to the cherry orchards of the Dean.

In 1888 these four houses in Lower Road were turned into shops. Holland's was a grocery shop, Alfred Barge was a pork butcher, King's were boot menders and Mrs Shackell ran the Thistle Hand Laundry. Notice how the shops still had gardens outside them.

Strand Castle, 1891. In the census of that year it was called 'Ye Tower by Ye Strand'. It was built by the eccentric William Grazebrooke, a retired merchant, who used a revolutionary concrete system and materials dredged from the bottom of the Water. Sadly it did not last, and crumbled away because the concrete was not reinforced. Ironically the building spent part of its life as an iron foundry.

'Ye Olde Strande Castle' camp site, 1950. Cookham has always been a favourite tourist destination, and in these snaps you can see children enjoying the simple pleasures of a holiday in the grounds of the folly. Note the see-saw in the picture below which certainly would not pass safety regulations today. Caravans and tents were available to hire and a small shop sold groceries.

The Methodist church, Lower Road. The foundation stones were laid in September 1904 by Mrs E.M. Worster and various members of her family. The iron gates and lantern are worth noting.

The late spring blizzard of 1908 in Lower Road. The building on the right advertising J. Frewing and Sons, builders and decorators, is now the Cookham Florist attached to Pinder Hall. On the left are the gates of the wheelwrights, where the houses of Coxborrow Close now stand.

Three

Up the Dean

Children in the Dean, *c.* 1900. Today's children would consider these boys and girls very overdressed. At the turn of the century hats, pinafores and stiff collars were everyday wear.

Dean Lane, Cookham Dean Bottom, *c.* 1917. Far from being the major route through the village that it is today, Dean Lane was then a small country track. Children from the cottages playing in the road had only to watch out for horse drawn taxis coming from the station and the occasional stray cow!

The post office, Cookham Dean Bottom, *c.* 1915. William Pryor was the postmaster at Cookham Dean Bottom. Robin starch and Cadbury's chocolate were just a few of the items on sale at the premises in Wells Cottages, known locally as 'Snuffy Row'. Although now a private house, the post box remains as evidence of its former existence.

The Chequers public house, 1905. This view is from the top of Well Hill, which is still visible today as an overgrown footpath. The men are enjoying the spring sunshine as they gossip at the site of the Bottom Well, a local meeting place. The fruit trees for which Cookham Dean was famous are looking magnificent.

The Bottom Well, also known as the Redan, at Cookham Dean Bottom, *c.* 1890. The girls help to wind up the bucket as the boys look on. It is said to be 100 ft deep and was the only source of drinking water for the area. It was closed in 1909. The tumbledown cottages were replaced by the Victorian villas seen in the photograph above. To the left is Spike Hatch, built in 1887, and on the right is Corner Cottage.

Dean Farm, at the junction of Alleyns Lane and Dean Lane, 1886. This was the home of the enterprising Jordan family who not only farmed but ran fly cabs and coal and milk deliveries. The girl and duck are reflected in one of the old village ponds, filled in by 1901 when it became a health hazard.

Reddaways Cottages, 1886. These were bought by H.W. Jordan who amongst his other skills was a master builder. He enlarged one cottage with old timbers said to be from the refurbished Cookham Lock. Cromwell Cottages are seen to the left; at one time they were used for storing potatoes for the farm!

H.W. Jordan and his wife Annie. He was born in Cookham in 1856 and went to London to learn his trade as a builder, returning after his marriage to buy land in Cookham Dean.

Cookham Dean Forge, thought to be about 1890. One of the cottages at the Forge was a small shop selling, as advertised on the wall, R. White's lemonade.

Cookham Dean Forge, c. 1919. Harry Crockford, plumber, farrier and general handyman, here stands outside the forge with his family. Residents still remember the sandstone grinder he kept round the back, on which he would sharpen shears and farm implements.

Cromwell Cottages, 1886. Smoke comes out the chimney as the girls play happily outside. Built in the early seventeenth century, they have survived to become luxury homes today.

The home of the Walters family in Warners Hill, 1887. In this delightful rural scene the road has yet to be developed. The ducks are probably making their way up to the old pond on Hardings Green.

Opposite Uncle Tom's Cabin, September 1887. These vanished cottages were on the land which is now the garden of Hill House.

Cartlands Cottage, Fag End Road, 1895. In what is now known as Kings Lane, the girls look over the fence into a beautiful garden. They are standing by a tree whose preserved trunk can still be seen.

A 'chocolate box' cottage in Dean Lane, *c.* 1910. This house had previously been a shop run by Edward Startin, after whom nearby Startins Lane was named (see p. 78).

The Cricket Common, c. 1905. Tars Platt, Quarry View and Orchard House look very much the same today. To the far right is the Drill Hall, which was built by public subscription in 1899 for a company of village cadets founded at the time of the Boer War. In 1926 it was sold to the Young Men's Club and has now been replaced by the modern Village Hall. The goalpost shows this was the home pitch for the football club.

Minside Cottage, the Cricket Common, c. 1890. From here, the road leads down past the Methodist Chapel and the chalk pit into Kings Lane. The view today is obscured by trees and undergrowth. Minside was home to the West family who went on to build Old Mins.

Old Mins, the Cricket Common, 1891. A brand new fence surrounds the garden and to the left is a beautiful cherry orchard. The well worn path across the Common leads from Wessons Hill and Cookham Dean Bottom. These tracks were filled in 1898 to make the cricket pitch. Notices put up to ask people not to damage the Green caused much anger and were immediately torn down. Commoners felt they had the right to go and do what they pleased!

The West Family in 1896 at Old Mins. Old Solomon is seen here with daughter-in-law Sara Lucas and her family Kate, Margaret, Edith, Nora and baby Walter in her arms.

View from the chalk pit between the wars. In the background is Mayfield, where Kenneth Grahame lived while he wrote *Wind in the Willows*. The large house in the centre is 'Tythe Barn' – now a children's nursery.

Children playing in Dean Lane, *c.* 1903. Royal Cottages and Quarry Edge dominate the skyline, a view now obscured by trees. There is little hint in this tranquil scene of the traffic which now makes cycling and walking so dangerous. The chalk pit was last quarried in 1929 when the chalk was used to build the causeway in Cookham.

The Hare and Hounds, *c.* 1903. Seen here in its original state, this is one of four public houses which served the village. It sold Wethered's ales which were brewed locally in Marlow. The landlord at this time was William Fitchet.

The Hare and Hounds, 1929. The thatched cottage and smallholding on the right are now replaced by housing, but the pub looks much the same today, although it is now called the Inn on the Green.

Vine Cottage, Dean Lane, 1908. The Copas family, who ran the Chequers pub just across the road, are pictured outside their home. Baby Tom sits on Hannah's lap, James holds Will and George (right) and 'P.J.' (Pryce-Jones, the local apothecary) has Alice and Annie.

The Chequers, 1903. Landlady Mary Copas with the pet sheep which ran riot, knocking a tap off a barrel and causing 36 gallons of best ale to flood the cellar!

Uncle Tom's Cabin, 1886. The cottage on the left was incorporated into the pub nine years later. The tree is now even larger, and is a familiar landmark.

Hills Lane, c. 1920. 'Didler' Wicks walks his horse and cart up the muddy track past Uncle Tom's towards Harding's Pond.

The Jolly Farmer and Noah's Ark Cottages. Shem, Ham and Japheth, farm workers' cottages, were finally pulled down in the early 1960s, having been empty since 1937.

The Jolly Farmer, c. 1891. Landlord William 'Buffer' Hatch and his wife Elizabeth pose in the porch way. The notice on the left is on a blocked up door, evidence that the building was once two separate dwellings.

The Bishop family outside Ham Cottage, 1893. From the left, they are Jane, Denis and Harry, with daughter Nellie in the front. Jane and her husband Thomas came to live in Noah's Ark Cottage when they were first married and Thomas was the last resident – only moving out when the cottages were condemned in 1937. Nellie can also be seen outside the school on p. 51.

Ben Bishop and his wife Elizabeth standing outside their home at Starlings Farm, c. 1883. Ben was farm bailiff to James Darby, Esq. and father of Thomas. The gun would have been essential for his work in the fruit orchards and the name of the farm would suggest the problem!

Cookham Dean church, *c.* 1907. The rose-edged path leads from the old vicarage to the vestry. The stone crosses on the roof have disappeared and the vestry has since been altered and enlarged. The lightening conductor was added in 1904, after the turret was struck during a fierce storm.

The interior of Cookham Dean church, *c.* 1910. This was probably taken during a flower festival. Note the old gas lamps and standards. The dado was finally completely painted over by 1963.

Cookham Dean school, *c.* 1903. Twins Agnes-Mary and Marion Elizabeth Usher stand by the newly planted tree, with their friend Nellie Bishop. These premises became a garage in the 1930s and they remain so today.

The Revd George H. Hodson, the founding vicar of Cookham Dean church from 1843 to 1869. A formidable Victorian character, this vicar was responsible for starting the school. When he took up the post he was told he was to be 'a missionary priest of the most notoriously evil parish in the Oxford diocese'!

THE REV. GEORGE H. HODSON, M.A., F.S.A.

A panoramic view of the school and old post office, 1900. The newly built infants' school, used for the first time on 9 January, had places for 120 children. Sheep are grazing on common land. A lot of negotiating and bartering was done to allow the school to be built at all on enclosed land. In the end this plot of land was 'swapped' for new common land in Furze Platt.

The class of 1935, Cookham Dean School. The children all look healthy and happy – the only difference is that nowadays they wear a uniform. The laurel hedge and railings are still in place.

Four

The Commons

Odney Common, 1928. Stanley Spencer, then aged 37, is sketching in one of his favourite spots on a lovely summer's day.

'Home to Sterlings'. Walter Higgs herds cattle back towards Sterlings Farm across common land by the church in Cookham Dean. With the sun on his back and his lunch in his bag he drives the cows from 'Rag-a-bags' meadow in Popes Lane, over the Village Green and on to Mr Darby's farm. The church lych-gate had been paid for by public subscription in 1882.

Widbrook Common, c. 1910. Cows enjoy an afternoon drink, just as their descendants do today. Telegraph poles had started to appear in the 1890s and at this date the gated road is still unfenced. It was not until 1923, when cars started to come through in increasing numbers, that the cows had to be protected by fencing them in.

The Thames at Odney Common, 1920s. This was a very popular recreation area for visitors and villagers alike. London cycle clubs were regular visitors and the river was full of punts and swimmers on any sunny weekend. In the 1920s, the boys' bathing costumes were very modest!

The Village Green, Cookham Dean. From 1899 the Green was used by the local cricket team for matches, which explains its modern day name of the Cricket Common. Here David Hatch prepares to roll the square.

Playing by the side of the old wooden bridge across the Fleet at Cookham Moor, *c.* 1903. The new causeway with its brick bridge was built in 1929 (see below). The magnificent earlier Crown Hotel is seen looming in the background.

The Causeway and bridge over the Fleet, *c.* 1940. The Hatch family walk towards Cookham, pushing the baby in the pram. The Causeway was built up with the final chalk quarried from the pit in Cookham Dean. The new brick bridge was built with money donated by Mrs Balfour-Allan as a memorial to her husband Mr Edward Kay. The Maidenhead Advertiser of Wednesday, 16 October 1929 reports '...the beloved donor laid the foundation stone on Saturday afternoon at 3 o'clock in the presence of an influential and crowded gathering'.

On Marsh Meadow, 1895. This is a Victorian culvert on the meadows leading down to the river. In May of that year attention had been called by the Parish Council to the foul state of all the ditches around Cookham and the owners were requested to clean them out.

The organ grinder poses with his monkey as the horse takes a welcome drink in the Fleet at Cookham Moor. The wagon wheels are getting a much needed soaking to stop the wood drying out and splitting. The geese, for which the Moor was famous, share the common with a grazing horse.

Tugwood Common, *c.* 1900. The early spring blossom frames a lovely cottage called 'Stilegate'. It is still as delightful today, although a few more houses have since been built in the neighbourhood.

Tugwood Common, *c.* 1880. The man is reputed to be Billy Pyke Carter outside his home on the common near the entrance to Quarry Wood. The summer foliage is almost covering his small thatched cottage. He was a gate keeper and it was his job to open and close the gate when required. There was one at Dry Cottage on the road into Bisham called Queen's Gate, and another at Tugwood Common across Grubwood Lane.

Five

Water, water everywhere!

COOKHAM FERRY

An etching of the ferry at Cookham. The first wooden bridge was built in 1840 and until then this ferry was vital for carrying not only people but horses and cattle too.

My Lady ferry, c. 1895. This flat bottomed punt crossed the river at the bottom of Mill Lane to Ferry Cottage at Cliveden. Taunt calls this 'the grandest reach on the Thames' and it has always been popular with fishermen and walkers. Here a photographer is taken across the river, no doubt to provide some of the pictures we see in this book!

Cookham Lock, c. 1890. Happy boaters on a summer afternoon enjoy a day trip. This cut takes you through one of the prettiest locks on the river back to the main stream and Cliveden Woods.

William Lacey's boat yard, *c.* 1880. His advertisement ran: 'Boats of every description Built, Housed, Repaired and Let on Hire by the Hour, Day, Week or Season. William Lacey has a commodious Boat House (the only one by the water edge in Cookham), with every convenience for the Building and Housing of Boats. William Lacey respectfully solicits a visit...'

The same boat yard during the flash floods in June 1903. This later became Turks boat yard and was made famous by Sir Stanley Spencer in his painting 'View from Cookham Bridge'. Here we see ferryman Fred Brooks wading outside his cottage by the bridge.

Cookham High Street, 21 November 1894. A major flood engulfed the Causeway and surrounding area. Mr W.H. Bailey, local artist and photographer, wrote in the local paper: 'The oldest inhabitants say they have never seen water go over the Causeway before – cottagers had to live in bedrooms and provisions were supplied to them from boats and carts by letting down a basket on a string. …The Royal Exchange seemed to be in a lively condition all through the flood and although the worthy landlord had to build scaffolding all over the floors and invited customers to enter in Venetian style he seemed to be doing a fair amount of trade…. His hostelry was for the time turned into The Pier Hotel for the village end of the flood.'

The Pound, 1894. Mr Bailey continues: 'The enormous force of water… was quite like the sound of a very big river weir as the waters rushed over the Causeway on the Moor.' Here, as the flood subsides the party has been inspecting the damage which would take 100 cartloads of chalk to repair.

The Causeway in flood, February 1904. Mrs Bird, the organist at Cookham church, wonders how to get back to her home in Berries Road. Moor Hall is seen on the right of the picture.

The Causeway, 21 June 1903. Mr Gold's car, thought to be a De Dion Bouton, needs to be rescued by one horse power after getting caught in a flash flood.

High Street, 1947. The staff at the International Stores take a break from mopping out the shop. Stock was destroyed as the cellar was completely overwhelmed. These premises are now the Cookham Arcade. This was the first flood since the disaster of 1894 to come over the Causeway and certainly the greatest flood in living memory.

High Street, 1947. The gentlemen's hairdresser stands surveying the scene outside 'The Quality Shop' which not only offered hairdressing but cigarettes, tobacco, stationery and a lending library service. The shop was run by Mrs G. Rutter.

High Street, 1947. Customers of Mrs Smyth's High Class Fruit and Vegatables (sic) had to walk the plank to pick up their groceries! These days, the shop is home to one of Cookham's upmarket boutiques.

The Pound, 1947. Mr Harold Aplin, manager of the International Stores, drives through the flood water on his way to work on his 350 cc Velocette.

The Moor, 1947. 'Hello, hello, hello – what have we here? Sergeant Hollamby and his constable get their feet wet in the course of duty. They stand surveying the water as it laps into the grounds of Moor Hall.

Six
In times of trouble

The old Cookham fire brigade, *c.* 1908. Billy Jordan and the team of horses.

The Cookham and District fire brigade at the station, Berries Road, *c.* 1930.

Les Emmett proudly stands with 'Sir Roger', the brigade's motorized engine, in 1935.

Eric Jordan, William Hatch and Fred Robinson, officers of the reorganized Cookham and District fire brigade, 1932. Eric Jordan broke his neck while taking part in a display by the fire brigade and become one of the first patients to use a plaster of Paris body cast. For many years the parish fire engine was actually kept in Holy Trinity Church and, in 1895, despite repeated requests, the Parish Council still 'respectfully declined' to take on the cost of maintaining it. By 1910, Mr Pinder-Brown, captain of the fire brigade, had taken out a lease on a building in Terry's Lane to house their equipment, which by 1919 included: 'Shand Mason Manual Engine, Acetylene Motor Lamp, Two Hand Lamps, Double Set of Harness (complete), Extension Ladder, Two Stand Pipes, 6 Nozzles, about 900 Feet of Pipe, plus Uniforms, Helmets, Belts, Boots, Axes etc.'

Rose Hatch in the fire station with a converted Wolseley, during the Second World War. The ARP helmets hang on pegs ready for use. The vehicle proves that necessity certainly is the mother of invention! Only two bombs fell on Cookham during the war, and others fell on Cockmarsh in an attempt to damage the river bridge.

The Cookham Dean Home Guard, 4 July 1942, winners of the Vanderfelt Challenge Cup. Arms folded and hats at a jaunty angle, they proudly pose in what is now the medical centre car park in Lower Road, Cookham Rise. Top row, from left: -?-, Dick Palmer, Ken Deadman, Arthur Cotterall, Fred Holland. Bottom row, from left: -?-, Stan Brooks, Cecil North, Victor Clark, Dudley Tomlin.

The Home Guard on manoeuvres. Helmets on, bags packed and gas masks ready for use, the flotilla patrols the Lock and Cookham Reach.

The Home Guard ran a nightly patrol on the Thames. One of their duties was to keep a watch on the river bridge.

Relaxing in the sunshine at the Hare and Hounds, Cookham Dean, *c.* 1943. Only the blackout curtain around the entrance shows any sign that this is wartime.

Cookham Rise school, 1917. The caption reads 'Cookham Rise Handicraft Centre. V.W.W. Approved by the War Office'. The school, opened in 1908, was the first non-selective secondary school in Berkshire.

Seven

Making a living

Above Dean Farm, Cookham Dean, *c*. 1900. Tucks and Jordans work together to clear the land.

Cookham Dean farmer H.W. Jordan, *c.* 1887. Pipe in hand, he proudly leans on a gate into one of his cherry orchards. In the springtime the acres of blossom made this area a major tourist attraction.

Off fruit picking, *c.* 1905. Soft fruit farming was an important part of the local economy. Cherries, apples, plums and pears all went to Covent Garden Market and the name of Cookham Dean was known throughout the country.

Winter Hill Farm, *c.*1920. Basket making employed many local people, and these sieves or bushels were made specifically for the soft fruit. Tom Copas, Jim Harding and Bill Copas stop work for a moment to smile at the camera.

Winter Hill Farm, *c.* 1930. Jack 'Fluff' Price sits behind the milk churn. The cart advertises his employers, Copas and Sons, and their promise to make daily deliveries.

The Forge, Cookham High Street, *c.* 1930. Thomas Emmett stands outside the smithy with his assistant Arthur Pearce. Mr Emmett was a master farrier and became well known for his lamp standards and fire baskets. Examples of his work can be seen outside the forge and are still around the village. Visitors today can enjoy a fine Indian meal in the premises which now belong to the Cookham Tandoori.

Haymaking at Englefield, 1919. Everybody helped out with the haymaking and perhaps once this photograph was taken they adjourned to the nearby Gate Hotel. The view from Englefield House provided inspiration for the artist Stanley Spencer.

Harvest, 1900. The Jordans' hay cart. Writing of when he was a boy in the 1930s, Norman Jordan recalls that 'the salad days for me were haymaking and harvest time. I was allowed to ride and drive the cart and bring it home to Dean Farm'.

Edward (Ted) Startin outside his shop, c. 1880. His thatched cottage was on Dean Road in Cookham Dean Bottom near what is now called Startins Lane. He sold tea, coffee, snuff and tobacco ('best shag 4d an ounce') and used old fashioned beam scales to weigh out coal.

Some of the Startin family. Ted's wife Jane stands behind daughters Emma, Rose and Laura. His sons became farm labourers and the girls went into service.

Startin's shop. Cookham Dean Bottom was at one time the heart of the village, with its well, pub, post office and shops. This shop was closed by 1903, and more recent housing now stands on the site.

Deadman's Stores, Bigfrith Lane, Cookham Dean, *c.* 1883. This was a very useful local shop. William Deadman, the proprietor, was a baker and grocer and dealt in hardware and corn. Hovis Bread is advertised on the shop window. He also became the postmaster. The barns on the left of the picture later became part of East's coal yard. The children are blackberrying just as our children do today.

Ricketts' shop, *c.* 1948. Miss Kath Ricketts stands outside her shop, the 'Enterprise Stores', on Dean Lane, opposite the Chequers. She sold fresh locally grown produce. Her brother L.J. 'Jim' Ricketts first ran a market garden and then became a well known local farmer.

William Taylor Deadman outside his bakery in Cookham Dean with his Trojan delivery van, *c.* 1912.

Shops in Lower Road, Cookham Rise, *c.* 1913. The shops, from left to right, were owned by Mr Charles Holland, Mr Alfred Barge, Mr George King and Mrs Isabella Shackell, giving rise to the local children's chant: 'Mrs Shackell went to Holland in a Barge to see the King'.

Norman's Paper Shop and Lending Library, *c.* 1949. Sewing patterns for evening and sports wear hang in the window and the Daily Sketch and News Chronicle headline the news of the day.

Chalfont's Cycle and Motor Stores, attached to what is now the Swan Uppers pub in the Pound. Mr Chalfont encourages customers to 'ride rigid rapid reliable Raleighs'. The early motor bike being examined in front of the shop is a Royal Enfield and Pratt's Motor Oil is obviously the mechanic's choice!

Hilltop Stores, Cookham Rise, 1900. On the corner of what is now Graham Road, the Misses Graham ran a drapery store. Hanging in the window you can see samples of corsetry and underwear. They also offered sewing machine sales and a dyeing and laundry service.

Eight

Time off

The Copas family with friends, *c.* 1925. From the left: Tom Copas, Laurie Burrows, George Copas, Annie Copas, Ralph Burrows and Will Copas.

Cookham Lock, Ascot Sunday. In Edwardian times Cookham was a favoured destination for day trippers, with Ascot and Henley being great occasions for dressing up. On the river it was the height of fashion to wear your Sunday best frock and largest hat, with the men wearing white trousers and boaters. The lock keepers would be kept busy from dawn till dusk by the hordes of trippers.

Cookham Regatta, c. 1910. The regatta was always a great social occasion and the perfect opportunity to enjoy company for a picnic. Here steam boats and punts crowd the banks and spectators hang over the river bridge. The bridge itself is decked out with lanterns. The regatta had punting, sculling and gondola races for both ladies and gentlemen and the whole evening would be rounded off with a concert and fireworks on the lawn of the Ferry pub.

Ladies' Bathing Pool at Odney, 1905. This controversial bathing pool was built in order that the ladies should be able to bathe in private. Sir George Young disapproved and is said to have pulled down a dressing tent and drained the water. The pool soon fell into disrepair and only a few remains can be seen today.

Odney Bathing Pool. The earliest record of a bathing pool at Odney dates to about 1770, and a hundred years later Sir George Young started the first swimming club to ensure there was no public nuisance caused. In 1903 the Odney Bathing Pool Fund was established to pay for the upkeep of the facilities and life-saving equipment. The swimming club was reformed in the 1920s and it proved a great source of pleasure to the locals, as can be seen here.

Skating on Cockmarsh, possibly 1895. There was a bitterly cold winter that year, with temperatures in early February rarely rising above freezing point day or night. This caused severe problems for many people and soup kitchens and hardship funds were set up for the poor. However, conditions were perfect for the lucky owners of skates and warm coats and great fun could be had just messing about on the ice.

Melmoth Lodge, The Pound, March 1900. The Stoke Beagles visit Cookham. According to the Maidenhead Advertiser of the day 'The Master Col. Howard Vyse was present and there was a good following…. The Party returned to Melmoth Lodge at about 4 p.m. and partook of refreshments kindly provided by Mr. A. Gilbey.'

Hunting pack in Cookham Dean. Hunting was a favourite sport amongst the gentry of the day and a pack of Berkshire and Buckinghamshire stag hounds was kept in Kennel Lane. There was also a large stag pen nearby. Even then it caused controversy, with much correspondence in the local paper about the cruelty of the sport.

Cookham Dean church choir outing, 1926. All aboard! The choir are ready for the off in their charabanc, all hats firmly in place. Among their companions is the vicar Herbert Hunt sitting towards the back of the bus.

Cookham Dean Quoits Club, c. 1892. At the time, the game of quoits was very popular and the Challenge Cup was classed as a 'very valuable prize'. You can see members of these teams holding the vital ingredients for a good game – the quoit to throw and the beer to drink. The shovel that Ted Tuck is holding has yet to be explained!

Cookham Dean Cricket Club on the Cricket Common, *c.* 1955. This was just a couple of years before they built their own pavilion after much negotiation with the National Trust and the Ministry of Agriculture and Fisheries.

Cookham Dean Football Club, 1920, the winning team in the Maidenhead and District Friendly League proudly pose with their shield outside Royal Cottages on the Cricket Common.

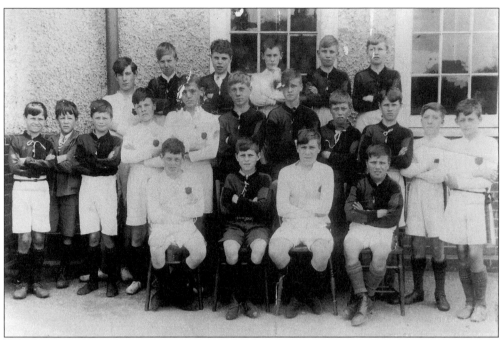

Cookham Rise Senior School football and athletics team outside the school building in 1927.

Cookham Cossacks speedway team, 1953. This bicycle speedway team used to practise on the golf course at Winter Hill and are here proudly showing off the 'Mars Trophy' awarded in the team competition at Slough Carnival. From left to right: Sydney Finlan, Philip Glennister, Peter Finlan, Raymond Fenner, David Cadle, Dicky Hunter, John Rutland, Michael Pocock, Roy East, his father the coal merchant Jim East and 'Bonner' Cadle. The young lad in the front row is David Matthews – now nationally famous for participating in the Scurry competition at the Horse of the Year Show.

Nine

Celebrations

The dedication of the War Memorial in Cookham, Sunday 21 September, 1919. It was built by public subscription. This scene was made famous in a painting by Stanley Spencer and as usual he included several of the villagers, including Kate Francis (now Swan), holding a bunch of flowers.

The Moor, 2 June 1897. Celebrations are in full swing for Queen Victoria's Diamond Jubilee. A large tent was erected and 600 visitors and residents were given lunch. 600 children were given medals. In the evening a procession by torchlight was followed by fireworks and a bonfire.

High Street, 14 July 1897. The Causeway and many houses were decorated with a great variety of flags and bunting. Gilbert Spencer describes how he and his brother Stanley headed the parade: 'It was higgledy-piggledy, this way and that, dresses dragging in the dust – just a straggle through the street of a thoroughly untidy and undisciplined-looking crowd.' He then describes the games on The Moor: 'There were three-legged races and the inevitable egg and spoon race, the eggs being dummies lent by Mr Hatch. With a tug-of-war and the National Anthem the proceedings ended and the children returned home, each carrying a rather misshapen Union Jack and a Jubilee Mug.'

The Chequers public house, Cookham Dean, August 1902. The whole village celebrated the coronation of King Edward VII and all the pubs did a good trade. Here you see the landlady Mary Copas standing outside her highly decorated pub, the flags and bunting making a very festive sight. Her son James is seated in the cart. Three lime trees which were planted to commemorate the event survive today: opposite the Old School House (now Sawfords), on Stirlings Green by the Church and outside Dean Farm. They were planted by Mr H. Edwards, Mr W. Lewington, and Mr H. Jordan. Mr Jordan's tree is the only one to have a plaque noting the event.

The Village Green, 23 June 1911. In the hottest summer in living memory a fête was held on the Village Green to celebrate the coronation of George V, with sports for the children of Cookham Rise and the Dean schools. Here the older villagers enjoy a tea party in front of Royal Cottages. Each child was given a bronze medal and a commemorative mug and trees were planted on the Village Green and by Woodlands Farm to mark the event.

The Cookham Coronation Festivities Committee of 1911. These notable dignitaries formed the committee who decided how the coronation of George V should be celebrated. Back row, left to right: Mr Alfred Flood, Col. Thomas Atherton C.B., Mr Edward Cooper, Mr William Spencer (father of Stanley), Mr Charles Shergold. Seated to the left is Col. Francis Cecil Ricardo C.V.O., J.P. with the Revd Alfred Batchelor M.A. D.C.L.

Cookham Dean Football Club, 1935. Proud winners of the Henley Town Cup in the Berkshire and Buckinghamshire Junior League, the team get ready for the parade to celebrate King George V's Silver Jubilee.

'Right royal' celebrations in honour of George VI on Coronation Day, 12 May 1937. At half past one, the children assembled on the Moor, many dressed patriotically as Britannia and St George. Even the bicycle was decked out in bunting as the procession wound its way from the Moor to Mr Jordan's meadow, Hillgrove, in Lower Road. The Webb and Jordan boys are part of the football team seen proudly holding a recently won trophy. Sadly grey skies and driving rain rather spoiled the day, but the pet show, baby show, country dancing and display by the fire brigade were enjoyed by all.

The Royal British Legion Women's Section at the coronation parade for Elizabeth II, 1953. During and after the war the Legion worked tirelessly to help disabled servicemen and their families and took part in many fund raising parades. Agnes Wetherall stands proudly in her nurse's uniform, flanked by Mrs Wilder and her daughter Sheila, Olive Mabbut and Lily Felstead. Mrs Bloomfield carries the banner.

The Police Station, Station Hill, *c.* 1936. Now called Elizabeth House, this is the home of the day centre for the elderly. Royalties from this book will help support their activities.

Acknowledgements

For their generosity in providing photographs, memories and encouragement we would like to thank:

Nellie Jordan, Peter and Ursula Fisher, Jay Lemon, Sue and Malcolm Wilkes, Tony Deadman, Harold Aplin, Gordon Badnell, Peter Barker, Patrick and Sonia Bell, Betty Bond, Alan Brant, Muriel Burley, Christine Cellund, Angela Cockman, the Copas family, Revd John Copping, Edward Dixon, Kathleen Emmett, Joan George, Keith Hatch, Fiona Jackson, Elizabeth Runnacles, Grace Shelton, John Shellabear, Eddie Smythe, John Spencer, Kate Swan, Agnes Weatherall, Philip and Dorothy Wilder, Miss A. Wilder, Cookham Dean School, Moor Hall, the Spencer family estate and Maidenhead Library. For help with photographic reproduction we thank Tim Rose of Martin Dawe Photography and Gill Harper.

The authors have tried to find the owners of the originals of all photographs used in this book to seek their agreement before including them. However, in some cases this has been impossible to do and we would like to apologize if any have been used without such permission. The book *Stanley Spencer by his brother Gilbert* can be bought from the Spencer Gallery in Cookham High Street.